KERRI,
GREAT T...
YOU BRF...
THE SH...

DOWNTOWN
FLIRT

FIRST POETS SERIES 19

Canadä

ONTARIO ARTS COUNCIL
CONSEIL DES ARTS DE L'ONTARIO

an Ontario government agency
un organisme du gouvernement de l'Ontario

Canada Council   Conseil des arts
for the Arts   du Canada

Guernica Editions Inc. acknowledges the support
of the Canada Council for the Arts and the Ontario Arts Council.
The Ontario Arts Council is an agency of the Government of Ontario.
We acknowledge the financial support of the Government of Canada.

DOWNTOWN FLIRT

PETER JICKLING

GUERNICA
EDITIONS

TORONTO · BUFFALO · LANCASTER (U.K.)
2019

Anna Geisler, general editor
Elana Wolff, editor
Cover and interior design: Rafael Chimicatti
Cover photography: FreeImages.com/Christian Sutter
Guernica Editions Inc.
1569 Heritage Way, Oakville, (ON), Canada L6M 2Z7
2250 Military Road, Tonawanda, N.Y. 14150-6000 U.S.A.
www.guernicaeditions.com

Distributors:
University of Toronto Press Distribution,
5201 Dufferin Street, Toronto (ON), Canada M3H 5T8
Gazelle Book Services, White Cross Mills
High Town, Lancaster LA1 4XS U.K.

First edition.
Printed in Canada.

Legal Deposit – First Quarter
Library of Congress Catalog Card Number: 2018954307
Library and Archives Canada Cataloguing in Publication
Jickling, Peter, 1981-, author
Downtown flirt / Peter Jickling.

(First poets series ; 19)
Poems.
ISBN 978-1-77183-377-6 (softcover)

I. Title. II. Series: First poets series (Toronto, Ont.) ; 19

PS8619.I29D69 2019   C811'.6   C2018-905003-9

For Wendy
and Bob
and Hannah

Contents

WINTER

(N)EARLY SPRING

FALL

AWL

The morning I leave
I ask for an awl to modify my belt.
My pants need torque
though I'm girthy:
a mystery.

My mom finds the tool
and atop a cutting board
etches a notch.
I eat eggs, watching.

The new hole looks small
so I plunge awl into leather,
twisting with gusto.
I've drawn blood doing less.
"Sweetie," my mom cautions:

An unexpected term
spoken an octave above
and a decibel below
her standard voice.
With a weight that confounds scales.

STREETCAR INCIDENT, UNIVERSITY & QUEEN

Amidst my Toronto loneliness
a geriatric's walker lurches into a disembarking woman.
"He rammed my legs with his cart," she whines.
"It was an accident," cry witnesses in unison—
"Don't worry about her."
He's acquitted; she's not.
The jury of passengers trades whatabitch smirks—
hacking her with ax-eyed verdicts.
She wears a yellow raincoat though there's no rain.
What burdens her?
Nevermind—it's fun now to judge.

LAST QUESTION ON THE TEST

You finish showering. Refreshed,
you stamp your torso dry.
You find unrinsed lather beneath your scrotum.
Do you re-shower, splashing your privates clean,
or towel off, hoping the soapy residue
and your afternoon sweat
won't chafe?
Answer with care, Sir.
Everything depends on this.

PICKLES

David hates pickles with moral ardor.
What knife cuts aesthetics from ethics?

FAILED REGISTRATION

"You new? Awesome! One piece of ID, please."

Wallet sifting.

"A health care card will do."

Worried searching,
left arm hunched like T-Rex.

In wallet:
Yukon library card, torn
hotel key card, unremembered
Montreal hospital admission card, 2007
University of Lethbridge student card, 2000-2005
business card, liquor store proprietor.

"Take your time, no pressure."

business card, digital print specialist
business card, watercolour painter
business card, financial advisor
dentist reminder, May 19th, year unknown
Tim Hortons Timcard, value unknown
twenty-dollar bill.

Not in wallet:
driver's license
health card.

"I hope you find them. Come back another time."

Epilogue: found them, other jeans.

THE WHOLE STORY

So yesterday I went to
register at a medical
marijuana clinic and I
realized I didn't have
a piece of legit ID in
my wallet.

But I had all this other
useless shit, some of it
was like ten years old.

I purged my wallet of all
the crap and all of a
sudden it was skinny and
didn't weigh much. Way
easier to forget.

Then last night I went with
a friend to a little rock n'
roll bar to watch a "freak
folk" band called Within.

Not really my taste, but
whatever.

When we went to a
different bar after the
show I noticed my wallet
was missing. I went back
to the original bar but it
was closed.

I was full of fear and
loathing and self pity, and
that's when I texted you.

Then I got an email today
from my friend and it turns
out the singer from that
band has my wallet.

Now I have to like her music
because she rescued my life.

CARPENTRY

Carpenters construct arguments from nails and wood—

enthymemes sound in proportion to craftsmanship.

Good carpenters master manifest logic.

FLAMES FAN, OCTOBER 2016

The Oilers will win the cup.
Not this year, perhaps,
but I read my knotty gut
and the alignment of stars.

LAUNDROMAT

I forgot *The Sound and the Fury* at the Laundromat
and returned twenty minutes later.

Life would be simpler without it,
but leaving things unfinished…

I found *The Sound and the Fury* where I left it
and remained ambivalent.

FIELD OF VISION (FOV)

When I study my FOV itself,
like watching the screen, not the show,
I see molecular phantoms.

Some look like cell nucleoli:
membrane and translucent center,
others scribbles,
others specks.
Some cross my FOV straight.
Others pivot,
others rest.
I've never seen two collide.

Do they behave differently when unobserved?
Do others see them?
What's their technical name?

Fuck the technical name.
I prefer molecular phantoms.

SHELTER IN TORONTO

Between my Parr and Margueretta Street sublet
are three days of limbo.
I check into the Kensington College Hostel
with kid-at-camp homesickness.

I slump awake the final night
listening to Augusta Avenue revelry—
preparing for an unfurnished room.

Upon arrival,
I lie on the floor,
backpack a pillow.
The subletee offers me her air mattress.
I name it Barry.

I place thirteen books
in three stacks
against the far wall.
Beside them, shirts.
Beside them,
an open suitcase
for socks and underwear.
In the corner,
a laundry sack.
I vow one act daily to mitigate the flophouse vibe.

Day 1: Move chair in from porch.
"Who doesn't enjoy a good sit?"
Day 2: Buy Barry a sheet.
Day 3: Plug in junior high clock radio.

It's not home.
But I slept nine hours last night
and made breakfast in the morning.

THE BALLAD OF OMEPRAZOLE

Coffee, hot sauce, sugar,
Philly steak and cheese.
Another shot of whiskey?
As many as I please!

They say I'm being reckless.
They say my diet's bad.
I've got a secret ally, friends:
my doc's prescription pad.

They call it Omeprazole.
It makes me far less pained.
It squelches indigestion,
keeps my reflux chained.

I've been warned of consequences,
heard tell of brittle bones.
To hell with osteoporosis,
it's onion rings I jones.

So every single morning,
I take my 20 mils.
Hooray for Omeprazole,
those gorgeous little pills.

SUNDAY NIGHT & MONDAY MORNING

Sunday night—
big week, Jickling:
Find housing and employment.
Swan Dive isn't free
and doubt doesn't assuage itself.

Monday morning—
clock radio: 9:58.
I stumble upright, stub my toe.
Like the drunk that drinks only after five,
I'm up before ten:
a go-getter, not a goof-off.

Pavlov winks.

SECOND LOCATION

After parting initial company,
I stroll an east-west artery
seeking another dive.
The bartender's eyes say, You've had a few.
Mine reply, I'll behave.

CRYING

I was the kid that wept at school—
until the end of Grade 8, when I said never again
and didn't cry for twenty years.

Infatuation and heartbreak came,
likewise insomnia, paranoia, body odor, Venlafaxine
and "Comfortably Numb" on repeat.
But tears didn't.

I tried—
head bowed, shoulders heaving
—but failed.

Then, summer's finale 2016:
Blasting through central Yukon in an '80s RV,
posse at hand,
I sob and sob.

Overwhelmed by pre-Toronto nerves and baked,
I receive kind words and worried looks
and feel better.

Then my Grade-8-self nudges me:
"Don't make it a habit."

WINNING AT COURT

Sometime in September I
got a double ticket for
speeding through a school
zone and outdated
registration. The speeding
was $115, the
registration was $143.

On October 12 I phoned
the court clerk to pay
my tickets, but there
was just one on the ledger.
She tried to cross-
reference the other one
any way she could. No
luck.

I paid my one ticket and
thought I caught a
break.

Then a few weeks ago my
parents say I have mail and
it's from the court saying I
owe for the second ticket, plus
they tacked on 28 bucks
because I missed my date.

I phoned the clerk
yesterday and said it was
bullshit and she got me a
new date today.

They patched me into
court on my cell phone
and the crown said she
was opposed to my
motion.

I gave my side of the story
and didn't even ask for
the whole ticket to be
quashed, just the $28 levy.
The crown relented.

A small victory. I'll take it.

POET'S LAMENT

I'm pretty fucking smart,
until I'm so fucking stupid.

OFF-WHITE

City stimulus tweaks me.
In Toronto, as in Montreal,
I become surer of myself—
a northern mouse aping urban wherewithal.
But there's mania in my swagger
and hyperactivity on credit is a dangerous indulgence.
So I devote days—and hours within days—to self-care.
I read, watch movies, drink water, breathe deeply.
I survey my sublet in plaid pajamas and striped sweater.
Once, eating Chinese in the Dufferin Mall food court,
the noise and the neon
came like errand boys to collect their bill—
The hordes! The hordes!
I limped nestward and stared at the ceiling.
Off-white.
Perfect.

WHAT I DIDN'T TELL THE BARTENDER

I liked you instantly
and I think you liked me.

When I blew a kiss
and you caught it
with vaudevillian flare,
I melted.

If you want to screw,
I'd give it a go
but I'd rather know you
than fuck you.
Still, you're beautiful.

Sorry,
I'm kinda drunk:
an earnest dork.

Also—
I really like your hair.

REHEARSAL

En route to Swan Dive
I unfold "Awl"
on 8.5 x 11
and practice inflecting
the first stanza's last line with
faint irony.

I imagine myself
as Tom Hanks on Letterman—
charm oozing!

But when the camera rolls,
I'm awkward:
an object observed,
a photon measured,
a neophyte nervous.

WINTER

HOUSE KEY

In Toronto
my house key
needs a designated pouch.

I'm a loser.
I lose things,
but habitual storage helps.

I choose the three-inch watch pocket
within the larger pocket
on the right leg of my jeans.

Nine times of ten my key returns there.
But when it's missing,
I panic.

I've always found it,
so far...
alarm spawning relief:

leaving me weary
but intact.

ORCHID

On the edge of the long white desk,
adjacent the open Venetian blind—
held straight by the metallic brace
fastened by plastic claws
at six-inch intervals...

stands the orchid.

I didn't notice it initially—
weird, since its six flowers are Byzantine-purple,
approximately.

It entered my consciousness
when I got an inevitable text
from my new subletee
saying I was fucking something up:

"Last night I had to close
the window, please don't
leave it open when you're
away for a longer time, the
orchid needs to be in an
environment that is above
20 Celsius."

I know about orchids from *Adaptation*
scripted by Charlie Kaufman.

They are rare,
precious,
delicate.
They inspire obsession.
Madness.

Now I must keep the thing alive—
a responsibility worsened because cool airflow,
indispensible to me,
apparently kills this pansy.

So I reason with it:

"I will strive to keep your Byzantine its Byzantiniest.
Your survival is my priority,
but please understand—
a stuffy room isn't pleasant."

I'm negotiating with a plant.
And losing.

YELLOW CORDUROY BLAZER

Arms scrunched,
buttons hanging,
elbows balding but sound,
cuffs worn like oft-folded paper,
lining shining.

Its wearer implies,
I'm a scamp,
but I can write a poem,
compose a song,
explain the Russian revolution.

I don it last,
before grabbing my poetry
and walking into the wind.

If it doesn't keep me warm,
maybe it keeps me brave.

It's just a jacket,
but it's not.
It was a gift.

FINGERNAIL CLIPPING OPTIONS

Clip left, leave right unkempt—
Odd look?

Leave both unkempt—
Symmetrical-ish.

Ask friend—
Strangely intimate favor?

Manicure—
How much? I'll check.

WAITING, DECEMBER 17

The interview went well I think.
Good, because Toronto is skinning me to a finish.
I followed up by phone.
I followed up by email.
We're overwhelmed, they said—
no decision.
So I wait:
declining ATM receipts like a college drunk,
remembering a friend's counsel—
"If your art is your priority, the universe will provide."
New-agey, sure—
but more comforting than a silent phone.

PEDESTRIAN

Dupont & Lansdowne:
Snow falls at night.
TV predicts 15 cm.

A westerly man says, "Poor guy,"
re: an elder shuffling north past the Dupont center-line,
blocking traffic.

His shoulders crowd his ears.
His chauffeur's cap sprouts matted hair.
His cane owns five claw-like contact points.
His feet step three inches.

A waylaid driver beeps.
The westerly man screams, "Let him cross."

A woman unrolls her window
and curses another driver.
The pedestrian's pace is unvaried,
his face indifferent.
He reaches the curb and continues
into the white and black.

BANANAS

Bananas have become a staple.
They're tasty, hassle-free, and healthy,
I'm told.

I like them green-tinged—
texture meaty.
But they're fine yellow and brown—
texture ignorable.

There's a peel on my desk,
my third today.

The compost is full.

I'M WRITING A BOOK

I told John I was writing poetry in Toronto.
He didn't understand
at all.
I was demoralized.
Then, epiphany—
I'm not writing poetry,
I'm writing a book of poems.
Thirty so far, more intended.
I'm writing A BOOK.
My mood
about thinking and drinking here
improved.
Reader, I hope you found this poem in a book.
If so, I bet the launch party was a hoot.

VANCOUVER ISLAND INTERLUDE

December 22
Meet parents in Victoria.
Lunch, Munro's Books, Al Purdy.
To Shawnigan Lake suite
in rental's backseat.
They get the queen,
I get the twin—
which wheels into the den.

December 23
Gift shopping in Duncan:
$45 in twenty minutes.
Coffee with folks:
I say I'm a filmmaker.
Dad says no,
I say yes.

Christmas Eve, 11 a.m.
Home alone.
Big flakes falling slow,
seven deer on lawn,
Vikings, Packers on TV.
I hear "Fairytale of New York"
and think it's about me.

It's not.

BOXING DAY ENNUI

Outside I see Douglas fir green.
As rain strikes the skylight,
I lie bare-chested
amidst ruins of white bedding.

Now I see nothing,
because I've closed my eyes.
I'd rather sleep
than find something red.

HAMILTON

Flight AC 1182 from Vancouver
couldn't land at Pearson:
freezing rain.
It docked at Hamilton,
sat two hours on tarmac,
and was de-iced at midnight.

The de-icing apparatus
loomed over the wing,
bobbing on a steel hinge,
its face an illuminated rectangle
spewing green sludge:
the grotesque offspring of
Jurassic Park's venom-spitting dinosaur
and Pixar's computer animated lamp
(the big one).

When the monster turned,
I saw its head was a basket
holding people
that sprayed the sludge.

I was relieved,
then disappointed.

FLAG

I marched through slush
to watch our juniors play USA
and saw a Canadian Flag, shredded.
The red was pink.

Some say tattered flags are tasteless,
but on December 31, 2016
this one was George Chuvalo—
pummeled but standing.

If old prizefighters are a blight,
so be it.

When I arrived Canada was down 3-1.
"It's not over yet," I whispered.

QUANDARY

I've adopted a devil-may-care financial attitude:
Debt in the service of poetry is
badass.

But yesterday a job prospect arrived.
After failed pizza joint applications
31 Yukon Government bucks an hour
sounded good.

Good enough to truncate my literary sabbatical?

I went to an open mic that night.
The weather was shitty.
So was I.
I was not a badass wordsmith,
but a pragmatist
considering the job
as I performed.

Today I made calls, texted friends,
sought perspective.
As I did,
I composed this poem
in my mind.
I couldn't help it.

So I'm staying in Toronto
as planned.
I'm a poet goddamn it.
Let bureaucrats quake at my sight.

MAN IN LIBRARY

Asleep on a chair,
unlit cigarette in his lips:

He flinches,
rubs his brow,
checks his watch.

"Only 3:50?"

He replaces the old cigarette
with a fresh one.

Why?

Questions go unanswered.
He falls asleep again.

FARE

To make bus fare
I grab change from my right pocket
with my right hand
and sort with my right thumb.

My right thumb and index finger
drop the proper coins into the left's palm,
which clutches the correct change.

My right hand stores surplus currency,
then pries open the left.

The left tips the fare into to my right palm.

Spasticity causes one quarter to fall.

I pick it up: ready for the bus.

BUS INCIDENT, DUFFERIN & DUPONT

The bus is crammed
or people aren't moving back
so it seems crammed in front.

I'm last on.
The doors close but the bus stays.
A beeping sound repeats.

"*I'm* standing behind the line," says a woman.
A white line,
three inches thick,
crosses the aisle diagonally.
Presumably by getting behind it
I'd stop the beeping and we'd leave.

I back up inches.
"Dude you need to get off," says line lady,
"there's no room."

I worry I'm creating an incident—
another stigmatized transit malcontent.
But the driver yells, "Everyone back,"
and I shimmy behind the line.

"There you go," she says,
her voice conciliatory (I think).

I attempt a defiant look
but her face softens
such that I likely conveyed hurt.

The bus starts:
anned humanity rolling south.

TOUCH WITHOUT CONTACT

The subway lurches into Christie.
A pretty South Asian woman stumbles towards me.

I ready myself,
but she regains balance
without contact.

We exchange wispy smiles like gifts.

And she leaves.

Weeks later I ponder her
and the inscrutable knowledge
we shared:

a small moment
writ large.

ORCHID II

Four of six Byzantine-purple flowers fell.
I watered them,
warmed them,
and they died on my desk.

Dead flowers in my care?
Typical.

But Internet says orchids shed flowers periodically
and new bulbs form.

Dejection begets anticipation.
I can only wait and watch
and water
and warm.

A caregiver
and botanist,
despite myself.

ROOMMATE

He knows Miguel Ferrer starred in a "Tales from the Crypt" episode with Teri Hatcher. He knows Gene Tierney contracted rubella during pregnancy and birthed a disabled daughter. He knows Gaston Gaudio won the 2004 French Open. "The most anonymous player ever," he says.

Once he asked, "Were you YouTubing the 1959 interview with Bertrand Russell at 3 a.m.?"

"I was."

He speaks with speedforce. No tangent left behind, no central point forgotten. I count the times he says "literally." I marvel at his cigar-like joints. I back away as his Schwarzenegger anecdote evaporates between us. Behind my door I decompress. But bedroom life is cloistered. I steel myself and return: "What were you saying about Arnie?"

I dig in

with strange affection for this strange man.

VALENTINE'S DAY

Ten years ago today
I ate diner breakfast
and stalked Westmount,
thinking of Wittgenstein and Laura.
Two cops stopped me:
erratic walking.

At the psych ward
a counselor said I'd get Valium for the boozing
and a shrink gave me Seroquel for insomnia.
I didn't get the Valium
and left.

Today I
drink coffee,
do dishes,
fold laundry,
eat vegetables,
glance back:

Wittgenstein and Laura are there—
with Montreal's winter wind.

(N)EARLY SPRING

CLEANING YOUR ROOM

It's Sunday evening and you've vowed twenty improvements. A ramen noodle receipt molders on the floor three inches from a piece of pink notepaper. You grab both with a single flourish. One improvement or two?

BUSKING

I busked in Kensington Market,
standing beside a men's wear shop
with twenty-six poems, double-sided,
and a stainless steel tip bowl.

I faked precedent
by adding my coins
before bellowing into grey pavement.

First reading:
23 minutes,
1 donation:
value unknown.

Ronnie's for a shot and beer.

Second set:
different order,
8-buck float,
2 donations:
$2.35.

I enjoyed
making eye contact,
reading like it mattered,
looking confident,
doing something new,
and becoming childlike.

To Ronnie's again,
and $3.25 getting home by bus.

SAM AND PETER CALL GIRLS

Sam and Peter
turn one beer into five
and call six Yukon girls
on speaker phone.

One talks while driving (illegal),
one is home, sick,
one is boarding a plane,
one might buy a taxidermy shop,
one is rehearsing *Evil Dead: The Musical*,
one has phone anxiety.

When Sam and Peter leave,
the phone is missing.
They agree:
"It must be here because
we called the girls with it."
Sam and Peter love them.

Hopefully one phones back.

GUITAR

When Ben visited Toronto
we ate cheese from the rind
and he stored his guitar.

For weeks it lay such that
my door, flung open,
missed it
by mere
mm.

Tonight,
on a whim (ineptitude be damned),
I played Ben's guitar
and stowed it further from the door.

BLITZ

Halfway through my third beer I get bored.

Between 8:52 and 9:03 I text nine people,
asking one if he's seen Hitchcock's *Notorious*
starring Cary Grant and Ingrid Bergman,
asking one how her album is coming,
telling one of my upcoming reading.

But others only get, "How's it going?"

Soon my countenance perks.
I juggle six conversations.

Less bored? Yes.
Satisfied? Not completely.

If they knew my impersonal method,
would they have responded?

Would you?

ORCHID III

I killed it.
I think.

PURGATORY

The Poet Laureate is reading tonight,
but the girl I asked couldn't go.
My nose is snot,
my head is lead,
the weather is cold,
so I stay inside.

Revolver
is paused 0:19 into "Hear, There and Everywhere":
a McCartney tune.

Bukowski: Born Into This
is paused in the mid-50s:
Hank just quit the post office (the first time).

A *Tale of Two Cities*
is bookmarked at 300:
Carton has blackmailed Barsad.

I trade these three all night,
adding a fourth
and fifth.
Finishing none.

The poet's reading is over.

TRANZAC

The Tranzac is the Toronto Australia New Zealand
Club though Aussies and Kiwis are rare. It's a boxy
two-storey affair at Bloor and Brunswick—a music
hall subdivided into three venues.

The Tranzac has all-gender bathrooms.

It has a chocolate almond dispenser that takes
loonies and a peanut dispenser that takes quarters.

It has ten beers on tap, experimental jazz, and a
Kubrickian room with burgundy drapes (eight feet
tall) and old chairs (ornate and haunted).

It has hippies, Saturday jams, and Monthly shows
by Vivienne Wilder.

It has budget deficits, bulletin boards, and rumpus
room Thursdays.

It has family-like employees and volunteers, a
Poster of Australian war heroes, and a heck of a
New Year's party.

It has free shirts for staff, a membership
recognition plaque begun and abandoned in 2011,
and collapsible blue chairs.

It has free rehearsal space, queer raves, and few
security problems.

I'm the security guy.

I guard the entrance and say, "Smoke over there." If
I feel like it. First-timers ask, "What is the Tranzac
anyway?"

"It's a non-profit organization," I say. That's true
but insufficient, like describing Charles Manson as
American.

I should say, "it's a state of mind: ethereal despite its
concrete."

CASTING

When someone I don't know reminds me of someone I know, I think, If they made a movie about the person I know and the person I don't know became a star, then the person I don't know could play the person I do. And vice-versa.

WAITING ROOM

The nurse
strides through
the sliding door
and calls "Peter"
and I grab my book
and walk toward her
but another guy
named Peter with a
bandaged elbow
beats me to her
and the sliding door
closes behind him
and I'm standing there
like an idiot
and a woman in a
wheelchair
is looking at me
or maybe she isn't
and I almost
make a joke
but I can tell
she doesn't care
and I sit down
and another nurse
strides through
the sliding door

and wheels the
woman away
and I'm left alone
with the smell
of illness
and my
infected
goddamn
foot.

BOTCH

The guy who filled my cavity
had a salesman's wink
and a dentist's scraper.

He called the assistants 'girls'.
He played calypso music while gouging.

Two weeks later,
my tooth still hurts like the dickens.
Did he botch the job?

I took an Ibuprofen at 4:30 a.m.,
but another pain lingers:

At first, I sorta thought he was cool.

SOME OF MY 10,000 STEPS

I'm catching up
to a
woman walking
her pug.
I'm two feet
behind.
She
STOPS.
I can't halt
my momentum
and will
pass her
exactly as
a couple,
hand-in-hand,
will pass her
from the
opposite direction.
The sidewalk
is narrowed
by a
garbage bin
on my right.
I pivot sideways,
slide between
the lady

and
the couple,
graze both
shoulders,
and don't
look back.

DOWNPOUR

I buy coffee
and walk to the Galleria Shopping Centre.
One raindrop hits me near the entrance.
Inside I spend $17 on
spinach, bananas, coleslaw, pasta, and sauce.

Outside potholes become ponds
and wipers earn their keep.

I walk home. Drenched,
the rain stops when I reach my door.
A downpour with my name on it:
just my luck.

But awe seeps into ego
like rain on denim,
and I remember:

We haven't colonized everything,
and clouds still teach humility.

If we listen.

POSITIVE THINKING

The black mattress cover
on my bed
highlights every
pube,
drool stain,
and cum drop.
Luckily,
no one cares.

CIGARETTE

I smoke my cigarette
&
listen to one podcast about
William F. Buckley
skinny-dipping
&
one about
a *Boston Globe* columnist
who writes open letters to his son
&
they're all smug Internet laughter
&
my hourglass expires
&
I despair
&
I put the butt in my wallet
&
go inside
&
phone Casey
&
cry.

RESIGNATION

Hey man, I can work
tomorrow but not on
Saturday. I'm actually
flying back to the Yukon
on Saturday afternoon. I
kinda hit a wall here. I'm
sorry to leave you in the
lurch. When I booked my
ticket I wasn't thinking
about shifts and only
later realized I was
bailing on work. I'm sorry,
man. Thanks for
everything. I'll be back.

SWAN DIVE

I'm hiding on the corner barstool,
sort of.

There is the Addams Family pinball machine
and there is the free pool table
and I've played neither.

I chase Jameson with beer
while Abra makes popcorn,
salted perfectly.

Seconds after meeting me
she asked about my left hand.
I explained: cerebral palsy,
and knew she'd be important.

I'm more tired now
and my ear hurts when I swallow.
I settle my bill,
regret the pool unplayed,
and leave.

SUBLET SWEEP

We have three brooms
and no dustpans.

I sweep together
grit and
orchid leaves
from my floor.

The orchid
in my care
didn't die—
it was only ill.

I use my hand
to put the big stuff
(clotted hair,
elastic bands)
in the garbage
and try
to sweep
the small stuff
onto an
envelope,
but much
remains.

So I open my door,
 look both ways,
  and sweep
   the leftovers
    out of my room,
     across the hall,
      and under the shoe rack.

SHITTY PIPE

I use my shitty pipe
when my good one
is lost.

The glass underneath
the bowl
gets really hot,
really quickly.

Now my finger is burnt
and I'm looking
under the bed.

BEARD

My beard was trimmed in Toronto
for twice the normal price,
so it became a playoff beard:
no pruning for the duration.

Instead of the Stanley Cup,
I played for poetry.

My beard is blond under the lip,
red beneath the chin,
and reddish-blond elsewhere.
It has greys.

During sleep the right side mashes into my face
while the left lights out for the territories,
causing asymmetrical mornings.

I don't love or trust my beard:
It hid a ramen noodle yesterday.

Today it will garnish the barber's floor.

SMALL ROOM

My new room's
east-west width
is six coat hangers.

My father measured it
while we assembled my bed.

My bed lies against
the south wall.
My closet occupies
the southwest corner—
one coat hanger from
the bed's western edge.

My desk rests beside
the bed's northeast corner—
flush against
the eastern wall.
It forms a right angle
with my dresser—
flush against
the northern wall.

The dresser's western edge
lies 1/15th a coat hanger
east of the door.

The area of my floor is
42 hangers^2.
My dresser occupies
1.5.

I might remove it.

Notes

The Whole Story: Repurposed from text messages.

Carpentry: An enthymeme is an argument in which a premise and/or conclusion is implied but not stated.

Shelter in Toronto: "Who doesn't enjoy a good sit?" is a Montgomery Burns quote from *The Simpsons*: Season 8, Episode 12.

Winning at Court: Repurposed from text messages.

Off-White: The line, "the noise and the neon came like errand boys to collect their bill," references Willard and Kurtz in the film, *Apocalypse Now*.

Vancouver Island Interlude: "Fairytale of New York," by the Pogues, featuring Kristy MacColl, is my favorite Christmas song.

Flag: Canada lost that game and lost to the Americans in the Final, 5-4 in a shootout. Shootouts are no way to settle a Championship.

Quandary: Dubious hubris.

Resignation: Repurposed from a text message.

Acknowledgements

I am grateful to the editors of the following publications in which these poems appeared:

Spread Letter: "Awl," "Shelter in Toronto," "Off-White," "Pedestrian," "Downpour," "Tranzac," "Poet's Lament," "Beard"

Acta Victoriana: "Bananas"

Sewer Lid: "Guitar"

Thanks to my family for the ever-present support. I couldn't have done it without you.

Thanks to my friends for the laughs and the love.

Thanks to Daniel Brennan for filming episodes of *Peter Jickling Reads What He Wrote*.

Thanks to William Rideout for the studio recorded poems.

Thanks to Sam Gallagher, Patrick Keenan, Scott Maynard, and Tom Pritchard for setting my words to music.

Thanks to James Dewar, Stanley Fefferman, Claire Freeman-Fawcett, Michael Fraser, Jovan Vuksanovich, Georgia Wilder, Bänoo Zan, Myra Bloom, Catriona Wright, Chris Oke, Ted Nolan, Marketa Holtebrinck, and the entire Toronto poetry community for the openhearted encouragement.

Thanks to my editor Elana Wolff, first for championing *Downtown Flirt,* then for improving it.

Thanks to Connie McParland, Michael Mirolla, and the entire Guernica team. Your faith in me is humbling.

Thanks to Rafael Chimicatti for the fantastic design work.

Thanks to Mo Whibley for capturing my essence, or whatever.

Thanks to Toronto.

Thanks to Whitehorse.

About the Author

Peter Jickling is a poet, playwright, and journalist from Whitehorse, Yukon. He holds a philosophy degree from the University of Lethbridge. His play, *Syphilis: A Love Story*, was first mounted in 2011 and subsequently toured Western Canada, winning Best Comedy at the 2013 Victoria Fringe Theatre Festival. In October 2016 he wintered in Toronto, where most of *Downtown Flirt* was written. It is his first poetry collection.

Printed in January 2019
by Gauvin Press,
Gatineau, Québec